Options Trading for Beginners

Options Trading for Beginners

How to Get Started and Make Money with Stock Options

J. D. Scott

DYLANNAPRESS

Copyright © 2015 by J. D. Scott
All rights reserved. This book or any portion thereof may not be reproduced or used in any manner whatsoever without the express written permission of the publisher except for the use of brief quotations in a book review.

Dylanna Publishing

First edition: 2015

Disclaimer

This book is for informational purposes only. The views expressed are those of the author alone, and should not be taken as expert, legal, or medical advice. The reader is responsible for his or her own actions.

Every attempt has been made to verify the accuracy of the information in this publication. However, neither the author nor the publisher assumes any responsibility for errors, omissions, or contrary interpretation of the material contained herein.

Neither the author or the publisher assumes any responsibility or liability whatsoever on the behalf of the reader or purchaser of this material.

Contents

About the Book 1
Introduction 3
Options 101 5

    What Are Options? 6

    Buying and Selling Options 7

    Advantages of Options Trading 7
        Leverage 8
        Risk Limitation—Hedging 8

    Disadvantages of Options Trading 9
        Levels of Risk 9
        Intrinsic Value 9
        Time Decay 10
        Taxes 10

Types and Styles of Options 11

    Call Options 11

    Put Options 11

    Using Call and Put Options to Make a Profit 12

    Styles of Options 13
        American Options 13
        European Options 13
        Exotic Options 14
        LEAPS 16
        Index Options 17

Option Prices and Valuation 19

    In-The-Money (ITM) 19

    At-The-Money (ATM) 20

Out-of-The-Money (OTM) 20
Intrinsic Value versus Time Value 21
Option Pricing Models 22
    Black-Scholes Model 23
    Cox-Rubenstein Binomial Option Pricing Model 23
    Put/Call Parity 24

Getting to Know the Greeks 25
Delta 25
Gamma 26
Rho 27
Vega 27
Theta 28

Getting Started with Trading Options 31
Options Exchanges 31
Options Clearing Corporation (OCC) 31
Opening a Trading Account 32
Placing Your Order 34
    Order Types 34
    Types of Fill Orders 35
    Timing Orders 35
Understanding Options Chains 36
Making Trades 38
Trading Tools 39

Option Trading Strategies 41
Simple Strategies 41
    Call Buying 41

Put Buying 42
Covered Call 43
Married Put 44

Spreads **45**
Bull Call Spread 45
Bear Put Spread 46
Calendar/Time Spread 47
Butterfly Spread 48

Straddle (Long) **49**

Iron Condor **50**

Iron Butterfly **51**

Naked Calls **52**

Collars (Protective) **53**

Strangle (Long) **54**

Strategies by Market Outlook **55**
Neutral Strategies 55
Strategies for Bulls 56
Strategies for Bears 56

Exit Strategies **56**
Closing Out 56
Rolling Out 57
Exercising Options 57

Sources of Information *59*

Online Resources **59**

Apps **59**

Newspapers, Magazines, and Newsletters **60**
Newspapers 60
Newsletters 60
Magazines 61

Tips and Tricks for Avoiding Costly Mistakes *63*
Conclusion *64*
Glossary *65*
    Index 68

About the Book

THIS BOOK is intended for beginning investors interested in learning about the ins and outs of options trading. No prior knowledge is assumed. The book provides a general overview of options, explains how they function, how they can be traded, when they should be traded, and their advantages and disadvantages. We'll also take a look at the variety of option styles and a brief look at some of the many strategies that can be used to trade options successfully.

By the end of this guide, you should have a good basic knowledge of what stock options are and how to use them.

Introduction

NOVICE, and even experienced, investors are often wary of investing in options. Many people view options as risky, exotic, and only for investors with large bankrolls. However, nothing could be further from the truth. Options are a great way for all investors, regardless of experience or risk tolerance, to expand their portfolios and make money in the stock market—whether the market is going up *or* down.

Options are the perfect vehicle for increasing your leverage, allowing you to turn a small investment into exponentially large rewards. They can also be used as an insurance policy, protecting your investments in case of a market downturn. In short, options are a tool that every investor should understand and potentially put to use.

In this book, you'll learn all the ins and outs of stock options, from basic puts and calls to more exotic straddles and spreads. By the end of this guide, you'll have a complete understanding of trading options and be able to put them to use in your own portfolio implementing both simple and more advanced strategies.

Included are many real world and easy to follow examples so you will be able to clearly understand each of the principles and strategies discussed in action.

Finally, we'll delve a little into the psychology of investing and its importance in knowing which way the market is going and how this can help you better time your investments for even more profits.

Read on to get started in the exciting world of options trading.

Options 101

THERE ARE MANY different options for investing and many types of financial instruments that can be used to accomplish your goal of making profits. One key financial tool that savvy investors and traders use is options.

As with stocks, options can make a person considerable earnings. They are, however, much more versatile and dynamic than stocks. How so? Well, when trading stocks there are really only two ways to make money. You can go "long" by buying a particular stock and waiting for it to go up in value and if that occurs you can sell it for a profit. The other way to turn a profit is to go "short." In this case, you sell shares of a company and buy them back later at a lower price.

Options trading is much more dynamic with dozens of different ways to make potential profits. Investors can trade options not only on stocks but also on currencies, commodities, and various indices. Many novice investors enter into the stock market without the proper education and experience. These investors are missing out on considerable earnings by not trading options on the above vehicles.

Options are available today on most stock exchanges and can be purchased through low-cost online brokers. Although trading options needs a well thought out and comprehensive approach, you can certainly make a profit if you are dedicated and committed.

This book will guide you through the various types of options and strategies involved and, hopefully, allow you to make considerable profits on your invested capital. Understanding options trading is important not only for sophisticated investors but also for beginning traders who want to strengthen their investment portfolio.

What Are Options?

An option is a contract that gives the purchaser the right, but not the obligation, to buy or sell an underlying asset at a specific price on or before a certain date. An option, just like a stock or bond, is a type of security. It is also a binding contract with strictly defined terms and properties.

Basically, a stock option contract may be in two forms: call options and put options. In both cases you have the right, but not the requirement, to either buy or sell the underlying stock for a pre-determined price. The pre-determined price is also known as the **strike price**.

An important feature of options, regardless of type, is the **expiration date**—a date when the option expires and becomes worthless. Before the expiration date, investors can hand over the option to someone else during the month in order to make a profit. However, due to time decay as well as other reasons, the option will lose value the closer it gets to the expiration date.

As an example, say on June 1, 2015, company ABC is trading for $10 per share. You could buy a call option on that stock that would allow you to buy 100 shares at a given time (say August 23, 2015) for $12 per share. Why would you want to do this? Well you may think that company ABC is underpriced and heading upward. So you buy your option and you wait. If 45 days later company ABC is now trading for $15 per share, then you can exercise your option to buy the stock at $12 and you have made a significant profit. If, however, company ABC is trading below $12 then you would not exercise your option and they would expire worthless. You have now lost your initial investment.

In option terminology, the **premium** is the price of the option contract. It is in constant flux based on market conditions and what the underlying security is doing. The premium is equal to the intrinsic value (the amount the option is in-the-money) + the time value (the longer the time left until the expiration date, the higher the value). When you sell your option, you must deduct the amount of the premium from your profit.

Buying and Selling Options

In option trading, you can either be the buyer or the seller of the option.

If you buy a call option, then you have purchased the right to buy the underlying stock (or other underlying instrument) at the specific strike price on or before the expiration date of the option. If you have purchased a put option then you have the right to sell the stock at the strike price on or before the expiration date. In both cases, you can also sell the option itself to another buyer or let it expire.

A different scenario is when you sell, or write, options. In these cases, you are obligated to fulfill the terms of the option contract should the buyer wish to exercise it. So, if you sell a call option, you will have to sell the underlying asset at the strike price to the buyer. And in the case of a put option, you would have to buy the stock at the strike price. If you write options then you need to understand that it is up to the buyer whether or not the contract is exercised and you must be ready to fulfill the terms of the contract. However, it is possible to buy another contract to offset your obligation and in this way you can exit out of the deal.

Advantages of Options Trading

Once you get a handle on option basics, you will discover that there are quite a few advantages to using them both to increase leverage and to hedge against potential threats.

Leverage

Perhaps the main advantage of options is the ability to make large profits without a considerable amount of upfront capital. This is due to the use of **leverage**. Financial leverage is one of the most significant aspects of trading in options. This factor can give an investor a bigger return while using a minimum amount of capital in the initial stage of investment.

For example, if you have $1,000 to invest with and you bought stock in company XYZ that is currently selling at $10 per share, then you would be able to purchase 100 shares. If the stock rises to $12.50 you could sell the stock and make a profit of $250 for a return of 25 percent on your initial investment. (For simplicity, we will leave out brokerage commissions in this example.)

In contrast, by buying options on the stock and using leverage your returns could be significantly higher. If you bought call options on the above stock with a strike price of $10 for $10 each, then you could by 100 options which would allow you to buy 1,000 shares of stock. If the stock rises to $12.50 then you could exercise your option to buy the shares at $10 and then immediately resell them for $12.50. In this case your profit would be $1,500 (or a 150% return) on the same initial $1,000 investment.

That is the power of leverage. With options, a trader can make investments without borrowing capital and can control a larger number of shares with a smaller amount of initial investment.

Risk Limitation—Hedging

Another big advantage of options is that they allow investors to safeguard their positions against fluctuations in price, especially when the investor doesn't want to alter the underlying position. In this way, options can be used to protect your portfolio against large price drops. This practice is known as **hedging**.

Here is an example of how hedging with options can be used as a risk management strategy. Say you own 100 shares of stock XYZ and you are concerned that it may be heading for a fall. You could buy a put option on that stock which would give you the option to sell it at the given strike price, regardless of how far the stock price falls in the market. For the price of the premium, you have insured yourself against any further losses below the strike price. This is a conservative strategy for limiting potential losses in the market.

Disadvantages of Options Trading

It is wise to weigh the potential risks of options against the benefits that may be gained before you decide to try your hand at options trading.

Levels of Risk

There are two levels of risk when trading options depending upon whether you are the holder or writer of the option.

As the holder of the option, your main risk is losing the entire premium that you paid for the option. If the option expires worthless then you are out your entire principal.

As the writer of the option, you are exposed to a significantly higher level of risk. If you are writing uncovered calls, for example, then your potential loss is unlimited as the underlying security could potentially rise very high.

Intrinsic Value

While purchasing a stock gives a certain amount of intrinsic value, with options it is quite different. An option that is currently at-the-money or out-of-the-money (these concepts are explored more in the next chapter) has no real intrinsic value. Its only value is its time value, which is constantly declining the closer it gets to its expiration date.

Time Decay

A risk that is unique to options is time decay. The closer an option contract gets to its expiration date the more it loses value. Once the option reaches its expiration date it will have no value unless it is exercised in-the-money. If the underlying security takes an unexpected turn during the timeframe of the contract, the investor will potentially lose all of the investment capital. Unlike with stocks, you cannot simply wait it out. For this reason, options are known as *wasting assets*.

Taxes

Another element to consider when investing in options is the tax implications of your trades. Since options are short-term investments they are taxed at a different rate than longer term investments. However, losses on options can also be used to offset gains in other investments, so they can work to your advantage in this regard as well. It is best to consult with a tax advisor to figure out your best strategy for tax savings.

The bottom line is that options trading can be used to leverage your positions and make significant profits. However, they come with their own set of risks and require the investor to be constantly on top of what is going on in the market. Due to their unique time constraints, they are not for investors who like to set and then forget their investments.

Types and Styles of Options

THERE ARE a variety of different types and styles of options available. This section provides an overview of each type as well as some basic terminology every option investor should be familiar with.

Call Options

A call option gives the investor the right (not the obligation) to *buy* the underlying stock, bond, commodity, or other instrument, at a specific price within the time frame of the contract. The specified price is called the *strike price.* An investor who is bullish on the stock, meaning he expects the stock to rise in near future or within the specific time frame, would buy a call option.

For example, say Investor A thinks stock XYZ is going to post high earnings next month and the stock is going to go higher. So she buys a call option on the stock for $20. The option contract specifies that she can purchase 100 shares of XYZ at a strike price of $100 within the next 60 days. If the price of the stock falls below $100, then she will not exercise the option. The contract will expire worthless and she will have lost the $20 purchase price. However, if the price of the stock rises above $100, say to $130, then she will exercise the option, buy the stock for $100, and then sell it at the higher market price. She has now made a nice profit.

Put Options

A put option is the opposite of a call option. It gives the owner the right (but not the obligation) to *sell* the underlying stock at a specified price (the strike price) within the specified time period. An investor who is bearish on the stock, meaning he thinks the stock price is headed downward, would buy a put option.

For example, say Investor B thinks stock XYZ is overpriced and will decline in price over the next 60 days. He buys a put option on the stock for $20. The contract gives him the option to sell the stock for $120 within the next 60 days. If the stock rises above $120 per share then he would not exercise the option. It would expire worthless and he has lost his initial investment. If instead the price of the stock drops below $120, to say $90, then he would exercise his right to sell the shares at $120 and pocket the difference as profit.

Using Call and Put Options to Make a Profit

There are a number of ways you can use call and put options. For example, suppose you think that shares of BankUS that are currently selling for $200 per share are underpriced and are going to go higher in the next couple of months. You don't have enough money to buy 100 or more shares of stock, yet would still like to make money from the rise in the stock. In this case, you could buy a call option on the stock, which would cost only a fraction of the price of the stock. So you buy the call option and you now have the right to buy 100 shares of the stock at $200 anytime in the next 60 days.

You might be thinking, how am I going to buy the stock in the next 60 days for $200 per share if I don't have the money? The answer is that you don't actually have to buy the stock in order to make a profit. If your instincts are correct and the stock price does rise above $200, then your call option will become more valuable. In other words, as the stock price rises, the value of your option contract also rises. You will be able to sell the option contract itself, instead of the stock, and make a profit. The higher the price rises, the more your contract will be worth.

This works the same way for a put option, except in this case you want the stock price to fall. As the price of the underlying security drops, the value of your put option will rise. The further the price falls, the more valuable is your option.

As you can see, by buying options, you are able to make a profit regardless of whether the stock is going up or down in price.

Styles of Options

The previous sections have given an overview of the two basic types of options, calls and puts. This section will help you understand the various styles of options available.

Most options that you will purchase will fall into one of two categories, American or European. These are sometimes referred to as *vanilla* options. The main difference between the two is when you can exercise the option.

American Options

American options can be exercised at any time before the expiration date. Most options on stocks and equity are of this type. These are also the type of contracts traded on futures exchanges.

European Options

European options can only be exercised on the expiration date defined in the contract. These types of options are mainly traded in the over-the-counter (OTC) market.

The values of the two option styles are calculated slightly differently and their expiration dates are also different. American options expire the third Saturday of the month, while European options expire the Friday before the third Saturday of the month.

Similarities between the two include the pay-off and the strike price. The pay-off, either for calls or puts, is calculated in the same way for both types. Likewise, the strike prices normally are the same.

Exotic Options

While the above two styles are the main ones most investors will be dealing with, there are a variety of more exotic option types to be aware of as well.

Bermuda Options

Bermuda options are in between American and European options. In this type of option you are allowed to exercise them on multiple dates during the contract period.

Barrier Options

Barrier options are different from the other types discussed so far in that in order for the option to payoff the price of the underlying security must cross a certain level. They can be either put or call options. There are four types of barrier options, which are outlined below:

*Down-and-Out Barrier Options: A down-and-out option gives the holder the right but not the obligation to buy (in the case of a call) or sell (in the case of a put) shares of an underlying asset at a pre-determined strike price so long as the price of that asset did not go below a pre-determined barrier during the option lifetime. That is, once the price of the underlying asset falls below the barrier, the option is "knocked-out" and no longer carries any value. Hence the name down-and-out.

*Down-and-In Barrier Options: A down-and-in option is the opposite of a down-and-out barrier option. Down-and-in options *only* carry value if the price of the underlying asset falls below the barrier during the options lifetime. If the barrier is crossed the holder of the down-and-in option has the right to buy (if it is a call) or sell (if it is a put) shares of the underlying asset at the predetermined strike price on the expiration date.

*Up-and-Out Barrier Options: An up-and-out barrier option is similar to a down-and-out barrier option, the only difference being the placement of the barrier. Rather than being knocked out by falling below the barrier price, up-and-out options are knocked out if the price of the underlying asset rises *above* the predetermined barrier.

*Up-and-In Barrier Options: An up-and-in barrier option is similar to a down-and-in option, however the barrier is placed above the current price of the underlying asset and the option will only be valid if the price of the underlying asset reaches the barrier before expiration.[1]

Basket Options

A basket option, also known as a rainbow option, is a contract in which the value is based on two or more underlying assets. The decision to exercise the option is dependent on the prices of all underlying assets.

Capped-Style Options

In this type of contract a maximum profit is established. Capped options contain a provision in which the option is exercised automatically if the underlying security reaches a certain established

---

[1] http://www.wikinvest.com/wiki/Exotic_Options_-_Barrier_Options

price. These types of options offer the writer of the option a maximum amount that can be lost.

Compound Options

These are basically options to purchase an option. Also called split-fee options because the holder must pay two premiums, one upfront and one if the option is exercised.

Look-Back Options

This style of option givers the holder the right to either buy or sell the underlying security at its peak (in the case of calls), or lowest (in the case of puts), price over a specified time period.

Asian Options

Asian options, also known as average options, are those where the payoff is subject to the mean (average) price of the underlying security over a specific period time.

Binary Options

Binary options have a payout that is either a fixed amount or nothing at all. There are two types: cash-or-nothing and asset-or-nothing. In the first type, the holder would get a fixed amount of cash if the option expires in-the-money. In the asset-or-nothing variety, the holder would receive the value of the underlying security. Also known as digital options, all-or-nothing options, and fixed return options. The advantage to this type of option is that the potential return is a known certainty before the option is purchased. However, once bought they cannot be sold before the expiration.

Forward Start Options

Forward start options start with an undefined strike price that is to be determined in the future.

LEAPS

LEAPS stands for Long-term Equity AnticiPation Securities. LEAPS are essentially the same as regular options except for the longer expiration dates. A LEAP can have an expiration date that is up to three years away. The advantage to this type of option is there is a lot more time for the underlying stock, and thus option, to move in the direction you want it to.

Index Options

In addition to purchasing options on individual securities, you can also purchase options on a stock index. These can be appealing because they provide exposure to an entire group of stocks. Index options are flexible and can fit into the strategies of both conservative and speculative investors, during both a bull and a bear market. Most index options are European style options.

Options Trading for Beginners

Option Prices and Valuation

THERE ARE several factors that go into determining the price, or premium, paid for an option. One of the most important factors is the current price of the underlying security.

Based on the current price of the underlying asset, an option is said to be either **in-the-money, at-the-money,** or **out-of-the-money**.

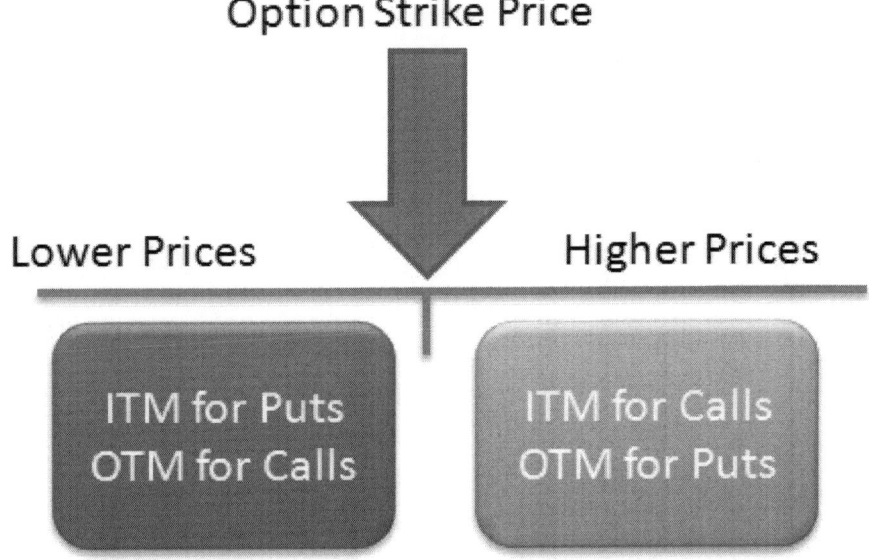

In-The-Money (ITM)

The phrase "in-the-money," means that your option currently has worth based on the price of the underlying asset. In the case of a call option, this is when the strike price is below the market price of the stock. For example, if a call option has a strike price of $30 and the stock price is currently $35, then the option is considered to be in-the-money

In contrast, a put option is "in-the-money" if its strike price is above the current market price of the stock. For example, if the strike price of the option is $35 and the stock is trading at $30, then the put option is in-the-money.

In either case, the larger the difference between the strike price and the current price, the more the option contract will be worth.

At-The-Money (ATM)

For both put and call options, if both the strike price and stock price are equal, then the option is said to be "at-the-money." For example, a call option has a strike price of $50 and the underlying share is trading at $50 in the market. At this point, the option has no intrinsic value. Its value is in the time value. The further away the contract is from the expiration date, the more time value it has.

Out-of-The-Money (OTM)

As you may have guessed, "out-of the-money" means the option contract has no worth based on the current price of the underlying asset. The holder of the contract would not exercise an out-of-the-money option.

A call option is out-of-the-money if the strike price is higher than the current market price of the underlying stock. For example, if the strike price of the call is $35 and the stock is trading at $30 the call option is out-of-the-money. In this case, the owner of the contract would not exercise his right to buy the stock at the strike price because it's cheaper in an open market.

In contrast, a put option is out-of-the-money if the market price of the stock is above the strike price of the underlying security. For example, if the put option has a strike price of $30 and the stock is currently trading at $35 in the market, then the option is out-of-the-money. It would not be profitable for the contract owner to sell the stock at strike price lower than the market price of the stock.

An out-of-the-money option has no intrinsic value but may have time value. However, its time value will quickly decay as the option gets closer to its expiration date.

Intrinsic Value versus Time Value

The option premium is composed of two major components—**intrinsic value** and **time value**. Intrinsic value is the difference between the market price of the stock and the strike price of the stock. It will be positive provided you are in-the-money and zero if you are either at-the-money or out-of-the-money. For an in-the-money option, the intrinsic value will increase as the difference between the strike price and the stock price increases.

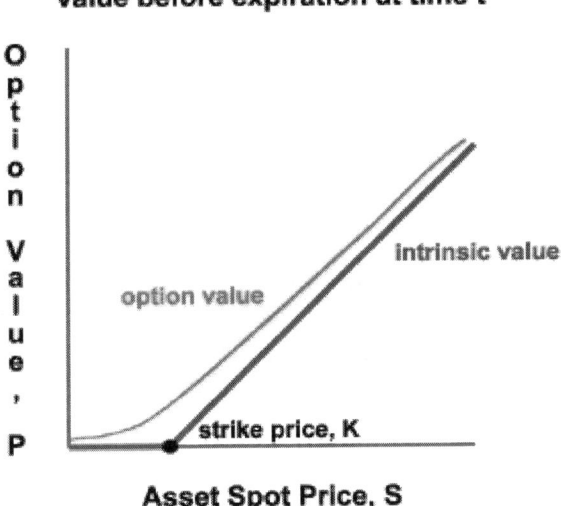

Intrinsic value is easy to calculate. For instance, if a stock was priced at $50 and you purchased a call option with a strike price of $45, then that call option would have $5 of intrinsic value. If, however, the stock price was selling at $45 or less, then the call option would not have any intrinsic value.

The other important component of the options premium is its time value. The time value of an option is directly related to the **expiration date**. This is the date on which the contract will expire. If this date passes and you, the holder of the contract, do not sell or exercise your option then the contract expires without any value. This is probably the main reason why options trading can be a high-risk venture.

To understand it more fully think of it as time decay. Simply put, the longer an option has before it expires the more time value it has. In other words, as time marches on, the value of the options you own will be losing some of their value—especially if the underlying security goes down in price or stays near the original price that you initially bought the options. Time decay is a critical element that must be monitored when you are investing in options.

Time value is a little more complicated to estimate than intrinsic value. Because of the fixed expiration date, there is only a certain amount of time for the underlying security to move in the direction you want it to. In general, the longer the expiration date is away from the current date, the more time value there is. As the expiration date creeps closer, the time value, and thus the premium, will decrease. This makes sense because if a security has more time to move in the price direction you want it to then there is more of chance that it could happen.

Option Pricing Models

There are several models that investors use to determine the current value of an option.

Black-Scholes Model

The Black-Scholes Model is probably the most used model for pricing options. It was developed in 1973 by the economists Fischer Black, Myron Scholes, and Robert Merton. This model is used to calculate the price of European options.

The Black-Scholes Option Pricing Formula

$$c = SN(d_1) - Xe^{-rT}N(d_2)$$

$$p = Xe^{-rT}N(-d_2) - SN(-d_1)$$

$$d_1 = \frac{\ln(S/X) + (r+\sigma^2/2)T}{\sigma\sqrt{T}}$$

$$d_2 = \frac{\ln(S/X) + (r-\sigma^2/2)T}{\sigma\sqrt{T}} = d_1 - \sigma\sqrt{T}$$

- S = Stock price.
- X = Strike price of option.
- r = Risk-free interest rate.
- T = Time to expiration in years.
- σ = Volatility of the relative price change of the underlying stock price.
- $N(x)$ = The cumulative normal distribution function.

As you can see, the formula for the model is quite complicated and most traders will not want to do the calculations themselves, but will instead rely on one of the online options trading calculators.

Cox-Rubenstein Binomial Option Pricing Model

This model is a variation of the Black-Scholes formula. This model uses the value of the underlying security over a period time, instead of just at the expiration date. For this reason, this model is often used for valuing American options which can be exercised at any time during the contract period. Again, calculating this formula by hand is probably not what most investors are going to do and a variety of online calculators can be used for this purpose.

Put/Call Parity

Put/call parity refers to the relationship between put and call options with the same strike price and expiration date.

Put-Call Parity Equation:

$$C + X/(1+r)^t = S_0 + P$$

C = Call Premium,   **r** = Annual Interest Rate,
P = Put Premium,   **t** = Time in Years,
X = Strike Price of Call and Put,   **S₀** = Initial Price of Underlying.

It is used only for European-style options. It states that "the value of a call option, at one strike price, implies a fair value for the corresponding put and vice versa."[2] Basically, the principle states that the options and underlying stock positions must have the same return. Otherwise, arbitrage, or the ability to profit from price variances, would arise and an investor could potentially profit risk free. Put/call parity is used as a simple test to see if options are priced fairly. Most online trading platforms offer a tool for analyzing put/call parity.

---

[2] http://www.investopedia.com/university/options-pricing/put-call-parity.asp

Getting to Know the Greeks

IF YOU TRADE in options, then you are going to be hearing a lot about what are collectively known as the Greeks. These values are used to evaluate various option positions and measure the risk involved.

Delta

Delta measures the option's price sensitivity in relation to the underlying asset. It is given as the number of points the option is expected to move for each point change in the underlying security.

This is the most used of the Greeks and it is important to know because it tells the investor how the option value will change based on price fluctuations of the stock.

Delta is usually expressed as a value between 0.0 and 1.0 for call options and between 0.0 and -1.0 for put options. They are sometimes expressed as whole numbers rather than decimals. The closer that Delta gets to 1 (or conversely -1) the more valuable is the option.

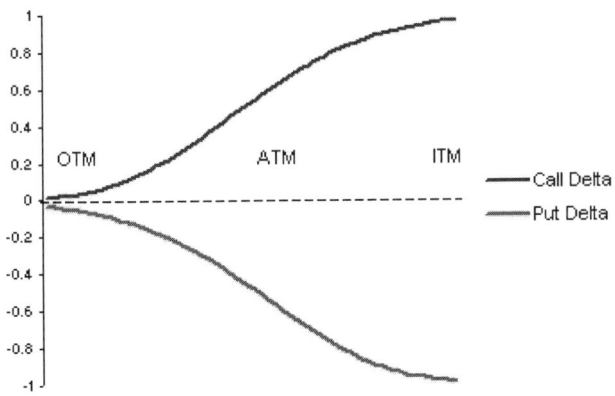

Options Trading for Beginners

Gamma

Gamma is a measure of how much the option's Delta changes when the price of the underlying asset changes. It is used when trying to assess the price fluctuation of an option in relation to how far in or out of the money it is. Gamma values increase as an option gets closer to being at-the-money. As an option moves further either in-to-the-money or out-of-the-money, the Gamma value will decrease.

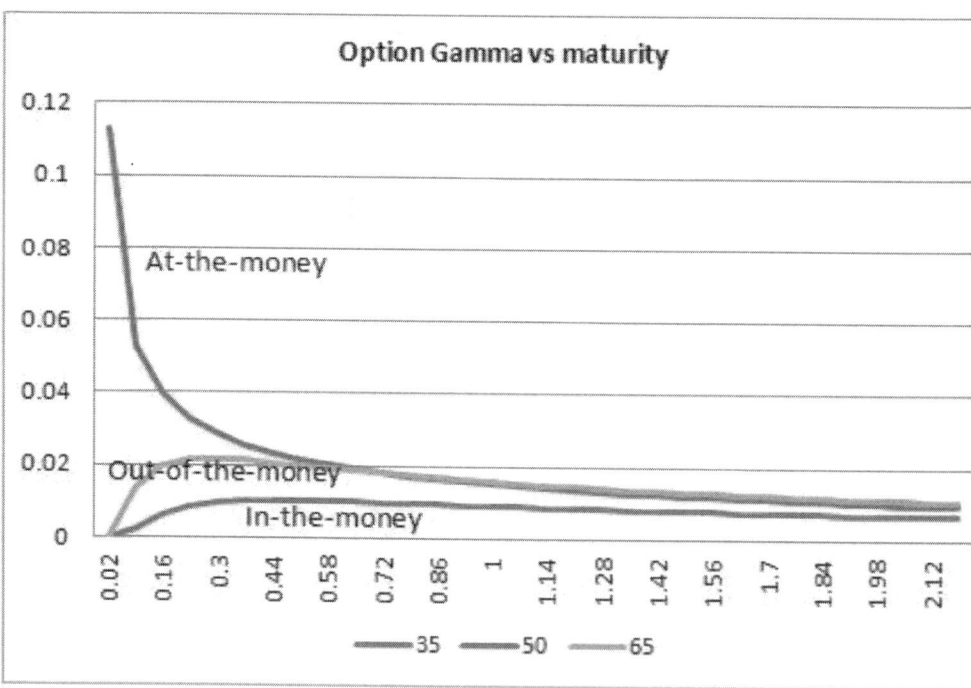

Rho

Rho is an estimate of how the price of an option, its premium, will change with respect to interest rate changes. Typically, if there is an increase in interest rates, then the premium on call options will rise and put option premiums will decrease.

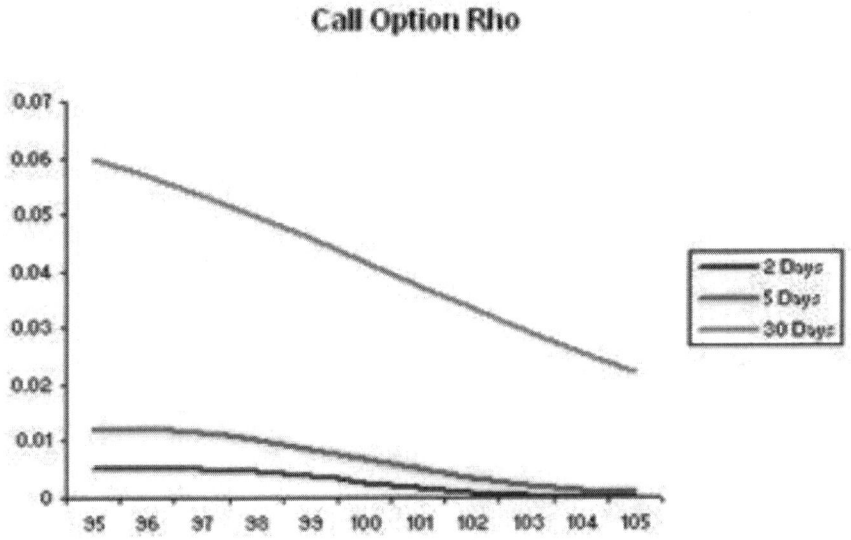

Call Option Rho

Vega

Vega is a measure of the sensitivity of an option to the volatility of the underlying asset. The more time there is to the expiration date, the more the option will be impacted by increased price volatility. Increased volatility will increase the value of an option.

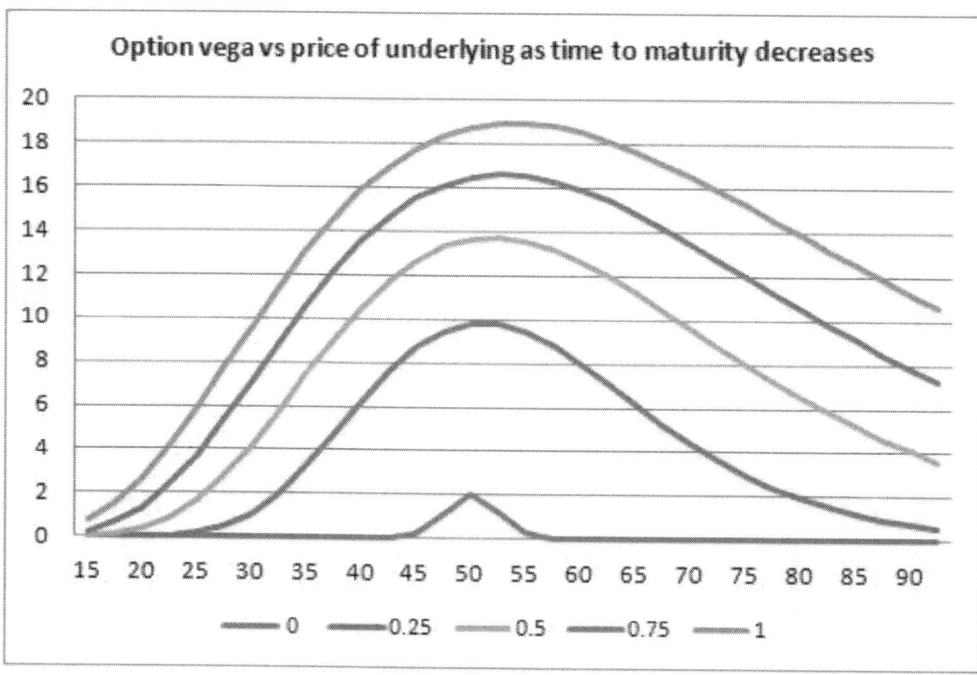

Theta

Theta is a measurement of the sensitivity of the option to time decay. It measures the amount of value that the option will lose for each day it gets closer to its expiration.

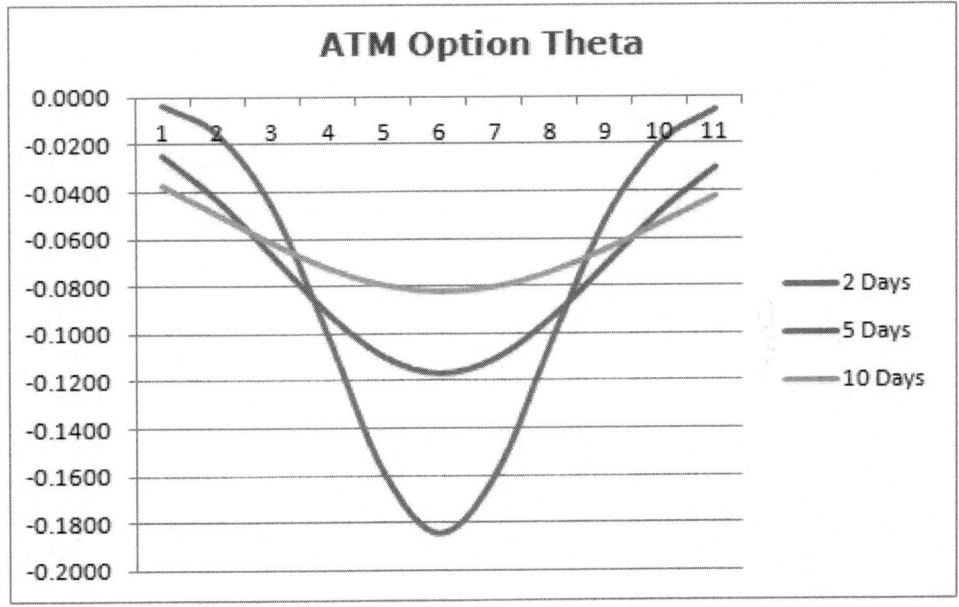

Most trading platforms provide up-to-date values for the Greeks for every option contract.

Options Trading for Beginners

Getting Started with Trading Options

NOW THAT you've learned the basics of options, it's time to get ready to make some trades.

Options Exchanges

Trades are made on one of several regulated exchanges. Most options are listed on multiple exchanges. Since option contracts are standardized, this means they can be traded between exchanges. The following are the current eleven options exchanges:

- BATS Options Exchange
- BOX Options Exchange
- C2 Options Exchange
- Chicago Board Options Exchange (CBOE)
- International Securities Exchange (ISE)
- MIAX Options Exchange
- NASDAQ OMX BX
- NASDAQ OMX PHLX
- NASDAQ Options Market
- NYSE Amex Options
- NYSE Arca Options

Options Clearing Corporation (OCC)

The OCC was founded in 1973 and acts as the clearinghouse for options contracts. It is the issuer and guarantor for options and futures contracts. Because of the OCC, investors can be confident that their trades will be settled, premiums will be collected and paid, and all assignments will be made according to regulations. It is under the jurisdiction of the Securities and Exchange Commission (SEC).

Opening a Trading Account

Before you can begin trading options, you are going to need to open a brokerage account. There are many brokerage firms available including both full service and discount brokers. What type you choose depends upon the level of advising you require. Discount firms offer lower fees but do not offer personalized advice. All of the top firms provide a variety of online tools and calculators to help you with your investing decisions.

Some of the top-rated brokerage firms include:

- Charles Schwab - www.schwab.com
- Fidelity Investments - www.fidelity.com
- TD Ameritrade - www.tdameritrade.com
- Interactive Brokers – www.interactivebrokers.com
- tradeMonster – www.trademonster.com
- Place Trade – www.placetrade.com
- TradeStation – www.tradestation.com
- OptionsXpress – www.optionsxpress.com
- OptionsHouse – www.optionshouse.com
- E*Trade – www.etrade.com
- Merrill Edge – www.merrilledge.com

Once you have selected your brokerage firm you will select your account type: either a **cash account** or a **margin account**. In a margin account you would use collateral to borrow funds to finance transactions. In a cash account you would trade with the available cash in your account. If you select a margin account you will be required to make a minimum deposit of at least $2,000 to open the account. A cash account typically requires either no deposit or a small deposit to open the account.

The amount of cash and assets you need to maintain in a margin account varies by brokerage house. If the amount drops below the required amount, then the firm will issue a **margin call**. This means you will need to add more capital to the account to meet their minimum requirements. If this is not done, then the brokerage firm will liquidate your assets. For this reason, it is important to be aware of your margin requirements.

Options Agreement

Once you've opened your account, the next step is to complete an options agreement prior to starting options trading. This agreement outlines your basic understanding of trading options, your financial capabilities to deals with losses, and your risk level. After you complete the agreement, the brokerage firm will assign you to an option approval level. While there is no official standard for what level you will be assigned, these are the typical levels:

- Level 1: Covered calls, long protective puts
- Level 2: Calls and puts
- Level 3: Spreads, straddles
- Level 4: Uncovered or naked calls and puts

Investors without a lot of experience will typically be assigned to level 1 or level 2. This is done to protect you from losing money due to limited understanding of the risks involved and also to protect the brokerage house against losses from underfunded investors who default on their margin accounts. In most cases, it is possible to have your level of trading moved up by contacting the brokerage firm.

Placing Your Order

Most beginners think that when they first start trading options it's just a matter of picking which options to buy and when to sell them. However, it's not that simple. There are four different types of orders that can be placed when buying and selling options. These four types are buy to open, buy to close, sell to open, and sell to close. After choosing one of these order types, you must also choose how to fill it either through a **limit order** or a **market order**. You must also let your broker know the timing of your order.

Order Types

Here is a breakdown of the different order types.

Buy to Open. The buy to open order is the simplest and most placed option order. This is used to buy an option contract to establish a new position.

Buy to Close. This is used to close out an existing short position and close the contract. You would place a buy to close order if you had short sold a specific options contract and wanted to get out of (close) that position. For instance if the options contracts you sold have subsequently gone down in value you can by these contracts back at the lower price by using a buy to close order thus locking in your profits. On the other hand, if your options that you sold short have gone up in value and you want to stop further losses you can place a buy to close order and buy the contracts back, thus preventing any further potential losses. Remember, if you have taken a short position, then you are making a profit when the price of the option has gone down, and you are in a loss position when the price of the option has gone up.

Sell to Open. This order is used to open a position on an options contract with the intent to short sell it. You would use this type of order when you are selling a covered call.

Sell to Close. The sell to close order is used to exit a position by selling the option contract. It is really just the order you use to sell options contracts that you already own. The order can be used for puts or calls.

Types of Fill Orders

After you have decided which type of order you want, you need to choose how to fill the order. The choices are **market orders**, **limit orders, stop orders**, and **stop-limit orders**.

With a *limit order* your trade will be executed at a price no higher (if you are buying), or no lower (if you are selling) than the price level you designate. This protects you from buying contracts at a price higher than you expected or selling at a price lower than expected.

A *market order* will fill the order at the current market price. This involves some risk because options can sometimes move quickly in price, which means that you could end up buying the contracts at a higher price than you were expecting or selling the contracts at a price lower than you were expecting.

A *stop order* will be filled when the price reaches the stop price. A *stop-limit order* combines the features of a stop order with the features of a limit order.

Timing Orders

When placing your order, you will also need to specify the order duration or timing. Types of timing orders are: day order, all or none, fill or kill, good until cancelled, good until date, or immediate or cancel.

The *day order* is an order that must be filled during the trading day that it is initiated on or it will be cancelled.

The *all or none order* must be completely filled or none of it is filled. For instance, if you are trying to buy 30 options contracts at a certain price but the broker can only buy 25 at that price, then the order is not processed. It is important to remember that this order remains open and does not expire at the end of the trading day unlike the day order although you can cancel it whenever you wish to.

The *fill or kill order* is like an all or none order with the additional requirement that it is cancelled automatically if it is not filled immediately.

The *good til cancelled order,* or GTC, is an order that does not cancel until you cancel it. Thus, this order will remain open until you decide to cancel it or it is filled.

The *good til date order*, or GTD, will remain open until a specified date and then cancelled if it has not been filled.

The *immediate or cancel order* is like the fill or kill order with one difference. With this type of order if some of it is filled immediately and the rest is not, the remaining contracts that are not filled are cancelled.

Understanding Options Chains

Options chains provide valuable information the investor needs to make trades. Most financial websites and brokers provide real-time options chains. Here's a brief overview of how to read an options chain.

J. D. Scott

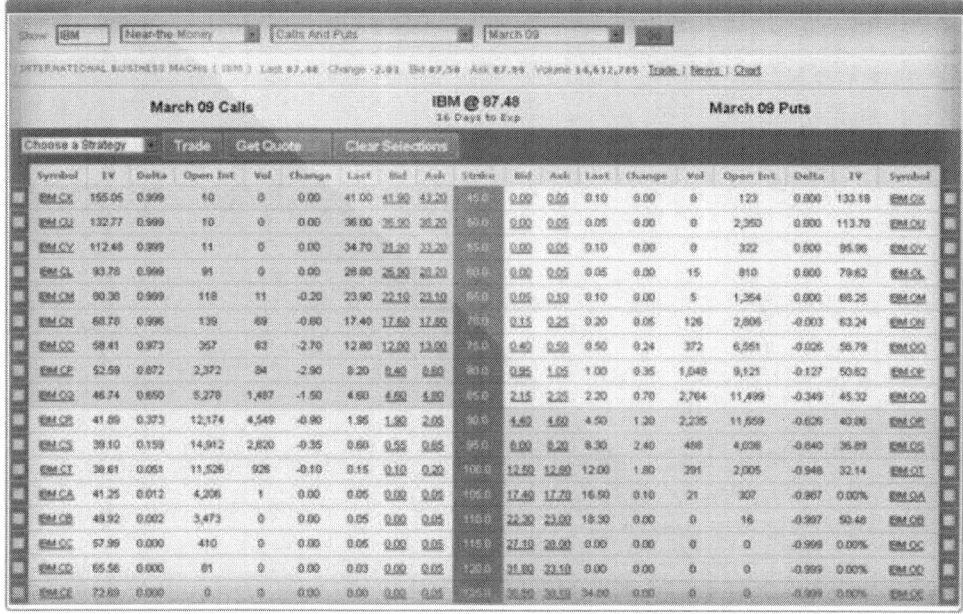

At the top of the chart is the name of the underlying stock, its ticker symbol, the exchange it's listed on, its current market price, and volume.

The columns in the option chain are: strike, symbol, last, change, bid, ask, volume, and open interest.

The first column lists the *strike price* for the given option.

The second column contains the *option symbol*. The chain displays information for both the call (C) and the put (P) for each strike price.

The *bid* is the current price that buyers are willing to pay for the option. The *ask* is the current price that sellers are willing sell for.

The *volume* is the number of options contracts that have traded that day.

The *open interest* column shows the number of outstanding open contracts.

Making Trades

The actual process for executing an order is pretty straightforward and follows the same process, whether you choose to trade online or over the phone.

1. Placing the trade

To place a trade, you will need the following:

- The option symbol
- The type of option: put or call
- The type of fill order: buy to open, buy to close, sell to open, sell to close
- The strike price
- The expiration date
- The price your are willing pay: market or limit order
- The timing of the order: day order, good until filled, etc.

2. Order confirmation

Before placing your order, make sure you check over all the information to make sure it is correct. Once you submit the order, you will receive a confirmation that the order has been placed. The order has not yet been executed. It is pending to be filled.

3. Trade execution

Depending upon your trade details, it could be just a couple of minutes or potentially hours or even days until your trade is executed. Once the order has been filled, you should receive a notification telling you the execution price.

4. Wait

Now you just need to monitor your positions and follow-through with your plan.

Trading Tools

Most brokers offer a variety of tools and calculators to help you with your options trading.

Research and analysis. Before you trade you will want to do some research and data analysis on the underlying stocks such as price history, volatility, earnings reports, and other data.

Paper trading. Before you part with any hard-earned cash, it's a good idea to try your hand in a simulated trading environment. Most online brokerage firms have tools that let you simulate trades and gain experience before you start risking money.

Options calculator. These tools will calculate potential profits and losses as well as provide values for the Greeks.

Options screener. Use these tools to narrow down your choices by screening options based on particular criteria such as volatility, market forecasts, or other conditions.

Options chains. This tool shows the entire series of put and call options offered on a particular stock along with their premiums, volume, and other characteristics.

Options Trading for Beginners

Option Trading Strategies

BEFORE YOU begin trading options, you need to have a strategy. You should know your investment goals and pick a strategy that will help you reach your goals. An investor who is looking to protect himself against potential losses on stocks he already owns will choose a different strategy from one who is trying to profit from the increased leverage that options can provide.

Simple Strategies

If you are a beginner when it comes to option trading, then starting off with a few simple strategies is probably the best way to start. As you gain more experience and become more comfortable with trading options you can move on to more complicated strategies.

Call Buying

Buying call options is a popular strategy for all levels of investors. In this strategy, you purchase call options on a stock that you believe is headed higher. If the stock price is higher than the strike price plus the premium paid by the expiration date then you will make a profit. If you are wrong, then you potentially lose your entire premium.

The majority of call option contracts are sold before expiration, when the premium goes up. However, you could also purchase the underlying security at any time before the expiration date if that is your objective.

To make a profit with this strategy, you need to have good timing and you need to know when you should exit the contract. If you wait too long and the stock does not rise high enough or fast enough, then the option may not be worth exercising or selling.

Some investors choose to buy call options instead of buying stock on margin. They offer the same use of leverage but carry less risk. If you have bought a stock on margin and the stock falls, you may get a margin call and be forced to add cash or liquidate assets to meet it. The only risk you face with buying call options is losing the premium.

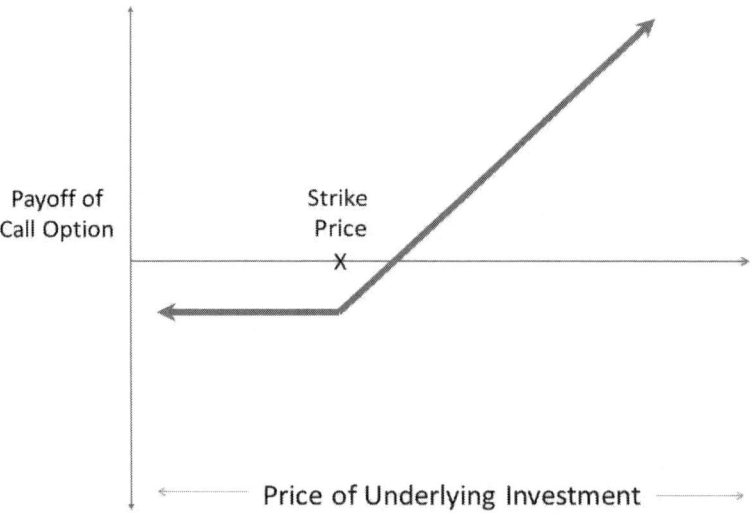

Put Buying

Put buying is much the same as call buying except in this case you believe the stock is headed downward. An investor would use this strategy as insurance against losses on assets already owned or to make a profit in a bear market. If you believe the market, or a particular stock, is headed down, then this would be a good strategy to consider.

This strategy is often used by stock owners to lock in a selling price and protect themselves against stock declines.

It can also be used for speculation on stocks that you don't own. As the price of the stock declines, the premium on the option should rise allowing you to make a profit. This can be appealing in a down market and is an alternative to selling stocks short.

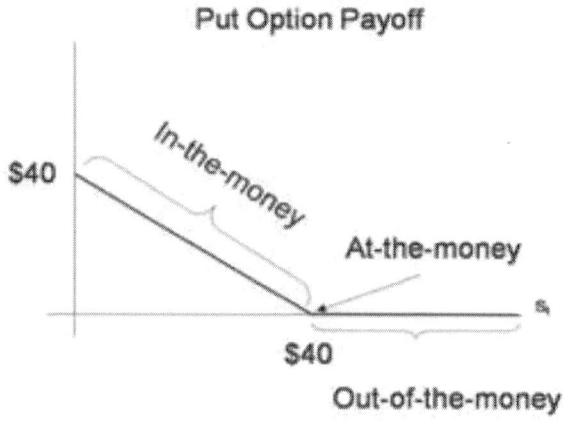

Covered Call

Another simple strategy is to write a covered call. In this straightforward strategy, you would sell (write) a call option for stocks that you already own, or purchase shares at the same time as you write the call, known as a **buy-write**. You receive cash in the form of the premium up front and your hope is that the call option is never exercised. An investor would choose this strategy to generate additional profits on a stock that she does not feel is headed higher, at least in the short term. In this way, the covered call acts as a dividend on the stock.

The risk with a covered call is that it will be exercised and you must be prepared to sell your stock to cover it. However, if the stock heads higher, you can protect yourself by buying a call in the same series as the one you sold and closing out your position. The premium paid for doing this should more or less equal the amount you received when you sold your original call option.

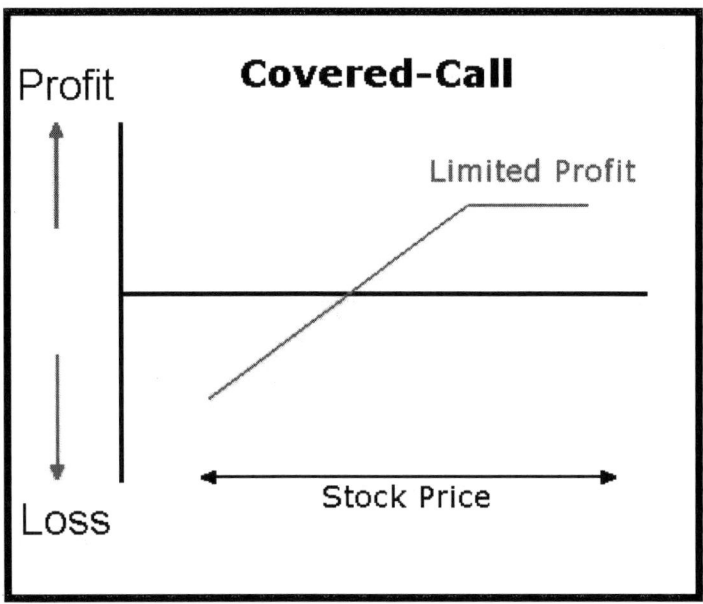

Married Put

A strategy in which you buy a put option on a stock which you already own (or buy at the same time as the put) is known as a married put. An investor would use this strategy to protect against losses if the stock price drops dramatically. It functions basically as an insurance policy.

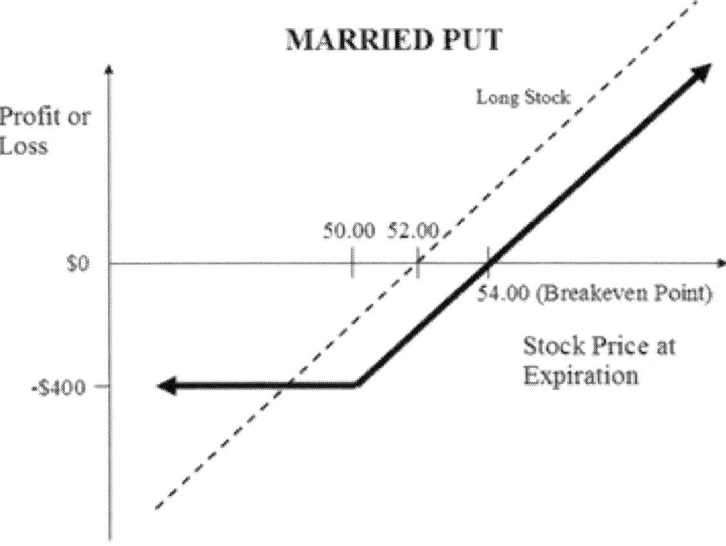

Spreads

A spread is a strategy that involves two transactions, normally executed at the same time. Spreads are a little more advanced than the simple strategies covered so far, but they are useful tools and well worth learning about. The most common type of spreads are **vertical spreads**, in which one option has a higher strike price than the other. In a spread, each transaction is referred to as a **leg**. The advantage of a spread is that your risk and potential losses are minimized. The disadvantage is that your profits are also limited.

Bull Call Spread

This type of vertical spread is used by bullish investors. The investor would buy call options on a stock at a certain strike price while simultaneously selling a call on the same stock at a higher strike price. Both options would have the same expiration date.

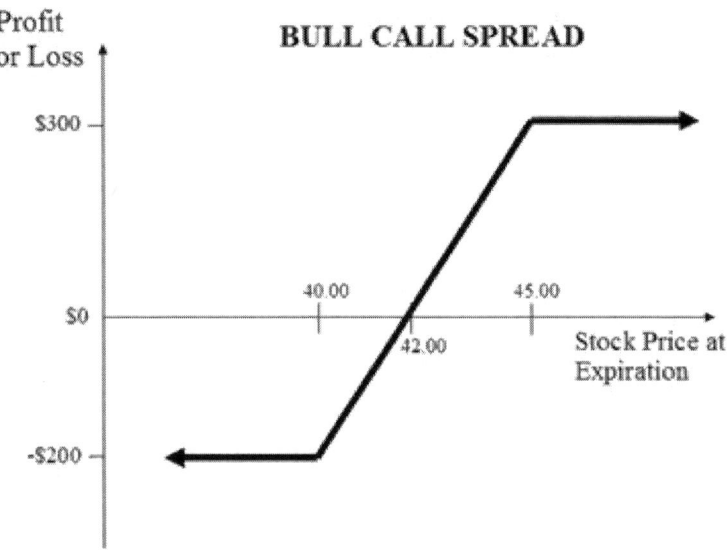

Bear Put Spread

This is also a vertical spread. In this strategy, you would buy put options at a certain strike price and then sell the same number of puts at a lower strike price, both on the same underlying stock with the same expiration date. This is a strategy for bearish investors who think the price of the stock is going to decline. Used as an alternative to short selling a stock.

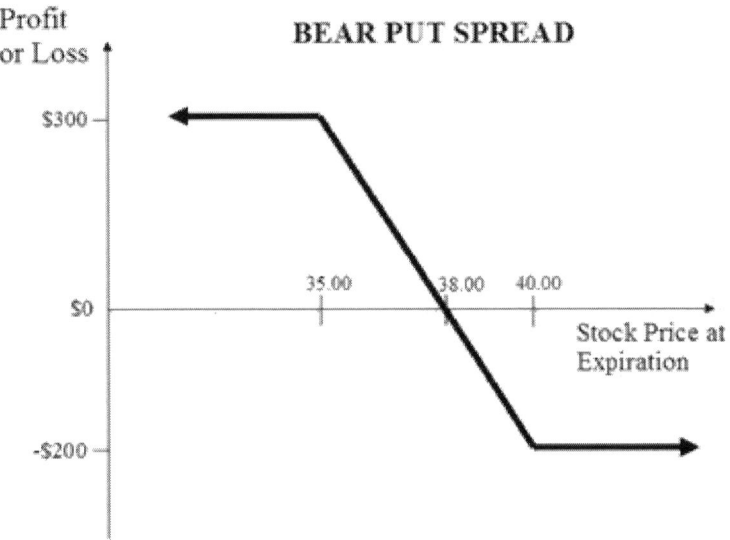

Calendar/Time Spread

A calendar, or time, spread involves purchasing an option with one expiration date and then selling another with a different expiration date. The strike price for each would be the same. In this strategy you are hoping to take advantage of time decay.

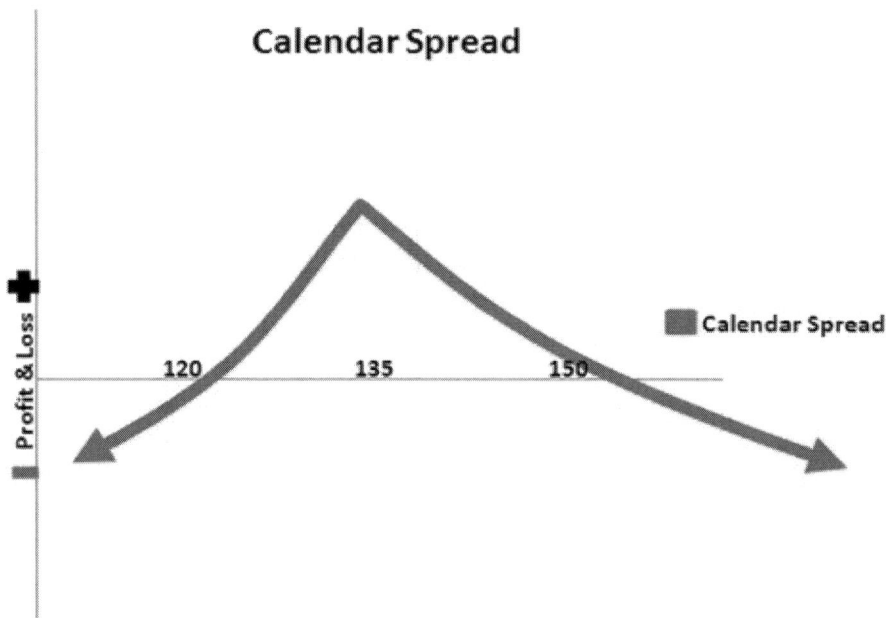

Butterfly Spread

Butterfly spreads are somewhat complicated and best used by more experienced investors. In this strategy, an investor combines both a bull and a bear spread strategy, using three different strike prices.

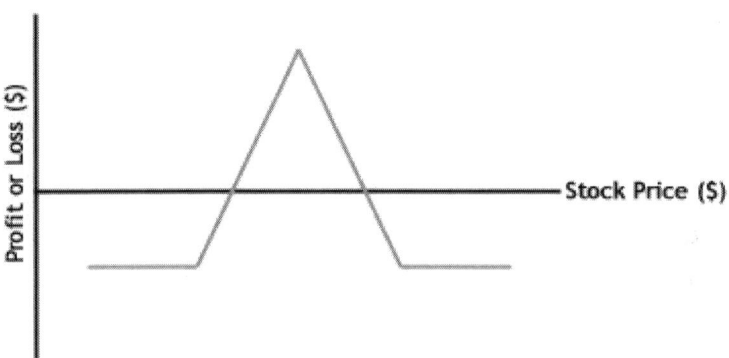

Straddle (Long)

A straddle is used by an investor who believes a stock is going to move significantly in one direction or another but isn't sure which direction that it is going to be. In this strategy, you would purchase (or sell) both a call option and a put option on a stock with the same strike price and the same expiration date. These offer unlimited profit potential while at the same time limiting risk.

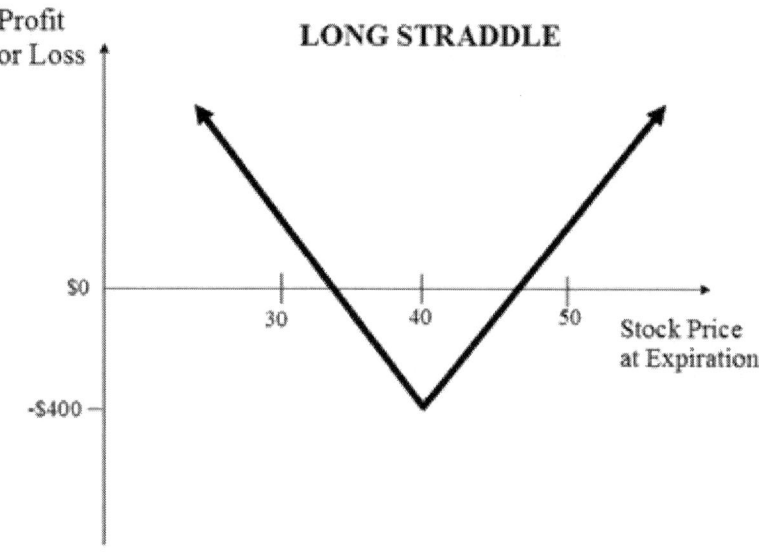

Iron Condor

The iron condor is a complex strategy that involves simultaneously holding a long and short position in two different strangle strategies. In this strategy, the investor sells an out-of-the-money put option, buys another out-of the money put option with a lower strike price, sells an out-of-the-money call option, and buys another out-of-the-money call option at a higher strike price. This strategy offer limited risk and a good probability of earning a small profit.

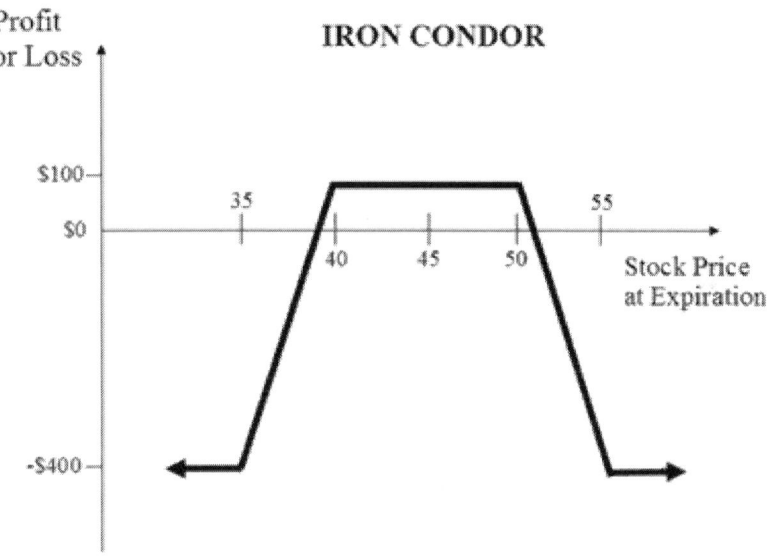

Iron Butterfly

This is another complex strategy used as a limited risk, limited profit combination. In the iron butterfly strategy the investor buys an out-of-the-money put, sells an at-the-money put, sells an at-the-money call, and buys another higher strike out-of-the-money call.

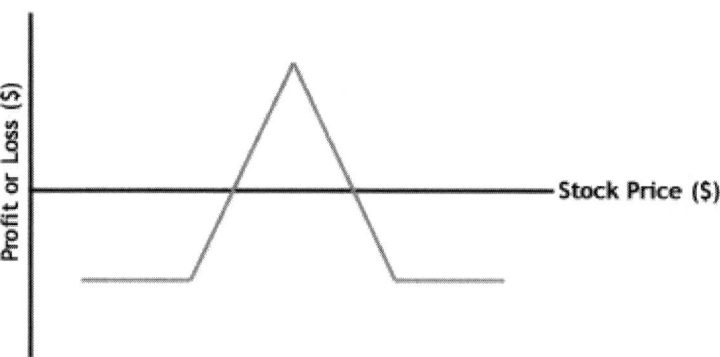

Naked Calls

A naked call is a risky investment strategy in which an investor writes call options on an underlying security without ownership of that security. It is risky because if the buyer of the call option exercises the option, then the seller must buy the stock at the current market price in order to fulfill the buyer order. The risk in this case is unlimited because there is no way to control how high the market price of the stock will go.

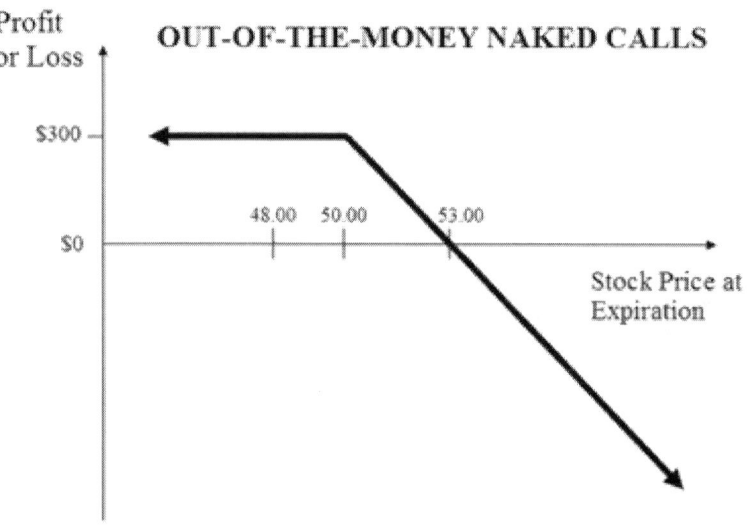

Collars (Protective)

In this strategy, the investor purchases an out-of-the money put option while at the same time writing an out-of-the-money call option on the same stock with the same expiration date. This is used by investors to lock in a profit without selling the stock.

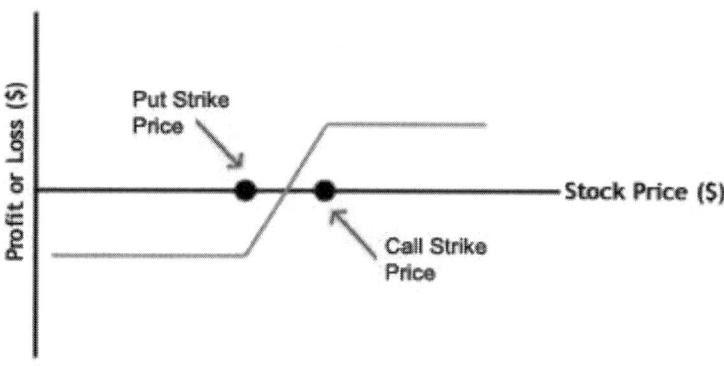

Strangle (Long)

In the strangle strategy, the investor buys both a put option and a call option, both usually out-of-the-money, on the same stock with the same expiration date, but with different strike prices. This is used when the investor is unsure which way the stock is headed.

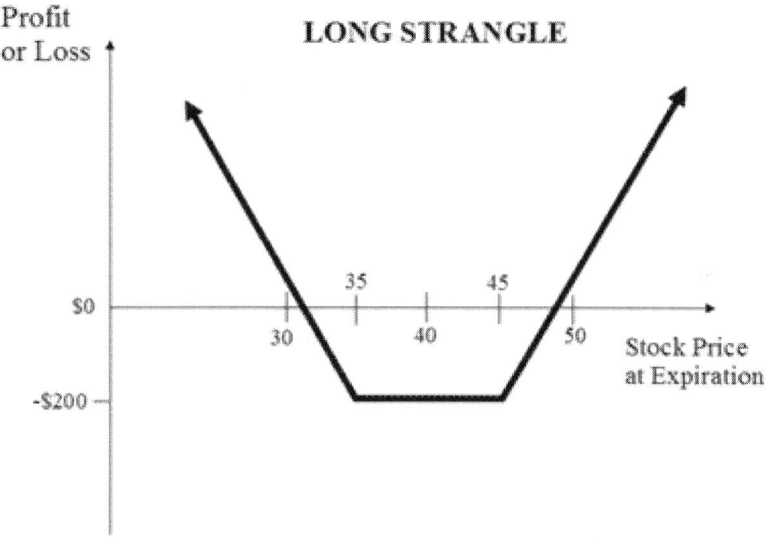

Strategies by Market Outlook

Below is a list of strategies to use based on your current outlook, either toward the market as a whole or toward a particular security.

Neutral Strategies

- Butterfly Spreads
- Calendar Spread
- Collar
- Iron Condor
- Married Put
- Straddle
- Strangle

Strategies for Bulls

- Bull Call Spread
- Bull Put Spread
- Collar
- Covered Call
- Long Call
- Married Put
- Short Put

Strategies for Bears

- Bear Call Spread
- Bear Put Spread
- Long Put
- Naked Call
- Short Call

Exit Strategies

It is vital to plan your exit strategy before you begin trading to avoid taking unnecessary losses. You can exit, or close, your position at any time before the expiration date. The timing of your exit is very important and can make the difference between making money and losing money. Before you begin, you should decide how you will exit if your option is out-of-the-money, at-the-money, or in-the-money.

Closing Out

One way exit to is by closing out your option. This is done by either buying an option you sold, or selling an option you bought. Basically reversing your position. If the premium has gone up since you bought the option, then you have made a profit. If the premium has decreased, you may want to cut your losses and sell.

As an options writer you are almost never forced to fulfill the obligation to buy the underlying security because you can close out your position before it is exercised.

Again, timing is everything when it comes to option trading and you must keep a close eye on your investments with regard to when it is time to sell, either to take your profits, or to cut your losses and move on. The closer you get to the expiration date, the more volatile the options become, and so you need to monitor them even more closely.

Rolling Out

If you don't want to close out your options, then you can roll them. This involves closing out your existing position and then opening a new position that is identical to the one you sold except with a new expiration date, a new strike price, or possibly both.

Exercising Options

If you are the options holder then you can choose to exercise your option and buy the underlying security. This typically only makes sense if the option is in-the-money, since in either of the other two cases it would not make sense.

If you are the writer of the option then you have no control over whether the buyer of the option chooses to exercise it or not.

Once you've considered the possible scenarios and chosen your exit strategies for each case, it's important that you closely monitor your positions and follow through on your plan. Options trading is fast paced and it can be easy to get caught up in the moment and lose track of your long-term goals. Don't let your emotions rule. Stick to your plan and you are much more likely to see your profits grow over the long term.

Sources of Information

RESEARCH IS key to being a successful investor. You will want find out as much information as you can about the underlying securities, the overall market, and the particular option series you are considering. There are a variety of good sources of reliable information available, much of it free of cost.

Online Resources

The Internet is probably the first source most investors turn to today for information. There are many great financial websites to choose from that offer plentiful up-to-date information and research. Here are a few of the best sites to get you started.

- BigCharts.com
- Bloomberg.com
- Financial Times
- MarketWatch.com
- Morningstar.com
- MSN Money/CNBC
- The Motley Fool
- TheStreet.com
- Wall Street Journal
- Yahoo!Finance
- YCHARTS.com

Apps

Putting technology to use can help you stay on top of your investments. There are several good investment apps that are worth checking out. In addition, most brokerage firms also put out an app.

- Bloomberg
- CNN Money
- Motif Investing
- Personal Capital
- SigFig
- Stock of the Day
- Stock Twits
- Yahoo! Finance

Newspapers, Magazines, and Newsletters

Newspapers, newsletters, and magazines are also popular sources of information. Most newsletters are paid services that offer information, picks, research, and recommendations.

Newspapers

- Barron's
- Financial Times
- The Wall Street Journal
- Value Line
- Washington Post

Newsletters

- Dow Theory Forecasts
- ETF Trader
- Global Resources Trading
- Hulbert Interactive

- MarketWatch Options Trader
- The Proactive Fund Investor
- The Prudent Speculator
- The Technical Indicator

Magazines

- Bloomberg Businessweek
- Consumer Money Adviser
- Fast Company
- Forbes
- Fortune
- Kiplinger's

Options Trading for Beginners

Tips and Tricks for Avoiding Costly Mistakes

SAVE YOURSELF some heartache by avoiding these costly mistakes.

1. **Don't invest more than you can afford to lose.** Remember, options trading is a risky proposition and if your hunches are wrong or your timing is off it is entirely possible to lose your entire investment. Start off small, no more than 10-15 percent of your portfolio should be used for options trading.

2. **Do the proper research.** Don't hurry into an investment because someone told you it was a good idea. Do your own research and make an informed decision before you make a trade.

3. **Adjust your strategy based on market conditions.** No one strategy is going to work in all markets. Keep abreast about what is going on in the economy and the financial world and adapt your trading strategies to match current market conditions.

4. **Know your exit strategy before you purchase.** Have a plan and stick to it. Don't let your emotions overrule your rational decisions. Choose your upside and downside exit points as well as your timeframe and don't let the euphoria of making larger profits sidetrack you.

5. **Don't take on more risk than you are comfortable with.** Every investor has their own level of risk tolerance. Know your risk comfort level and choose strategies that stay within that territory. You don't want to lose sleep at night wondering if you've made the right investment decisions.

Conclusion

YOU SHOULD now have a basic understanding to options and the world of options trading.

Now you are ready to apply what you have learned and get started in investing.

Remember, do your research and don't take on more risk than you are comfortable with.

Best of luck!

Glossary

American options: A type of option that can be exercised at any point up until the expiration date.

Ask: The current price that a seller is willing to accept.

At-the money (ATM): When the stock price is equal to the strike price of the option.

Bid: The current price that a buyer is willing to pay.

Break-even point: The price the stock must reach in order for the option to result in neither a profit or a loss.

Call: An option contract that gives the owner of the option the right to buy the underlying security at the predetermined price.

Close: To buy or sell an option in order to offset a previous position.

Collar: A simultaneous purchase of a protective put and writing of a covered call.

Day order: An order that must be filled on that trading day or it is cancelled.

European options: A type of option that can only be exercised at expiration.

Exercise: To invoke the rights granted to the option holder, specifically, the ability to buy or sell the underlying stock.

Expiration date: The date upon which both the option, and the right to exercise the option, expires.

Good 'til canceled (GTC): An order that remains open and valid until it's either filled or you cancel it.

Historical volatility: The fluctuation trends during a time span of one year.

Implied volatility: This is determined by looking at the historical volatility in order to estimate possible future volatility.

In-the-money (ITM): A call option is in-the-money if the strike price is less than the market price of the underlying security. A put option is in-the-money if the strike price is greater than the market price of the underlying security.

Intrinsic value: The value of the option if exercised.

Leverage: To use a small amount of money to control a much larger investment.

Limit order: An order that can only be filled at a given price or better.

Long: A position where you own a security or option.

Long-term Equity AnticiPation Securities (LEAPS): Options whose expiration dates are between 1 and 3 years in the future.

Market order: An order in which the buyer is willing to pay the current market price.

Naked call: A call option written on a security that you do not own.

Out-of-the-money (OTM): A call option is out-of-the-money if the strike price is greater than the market price of the underlying security. A put option is out-of-the-money if the strike price is less than the market price of the underlying security.

Premium: The price that the investor pays for the option.

Put: An option contract that gives the owner the right of selling the underlying security at the predetermined price.

Quadruple witching day: The third Friday of the last month in each quarter (March, June, September, December). This is the day that stock options, stock index options, stock index futures, and single stock futures all expire. Historically, these are heavily traded days.

Short: A position in which the investor sells, or writes, the option.

Spread: A strategy in which the investor holds two or more simultaneous positions. May also refer to the difference between the bid and the ask price.

Stop-loss order: An order to sell an option when it reaches a specific price level.

Strike price: The strike price, also known as the exercise price, is the predetermined price at which the owner of an option can buy (call) or sell (put) the underlying stock or other commodity.

Time value: The value left after the intrinsic value is deducted from the option price. Loses value, or decays, the closer it gets to the expiration date.

Volatility: The fluctuation in the option price.

Write: To sell an option to open a new position.

Index

A
all or none order, 36
American options, 13–14
apps, 58–60
ask, 37
Asoan options, 16
at-the-money (ATM), 20

B
barrier options, 14–15
basket options, 15
bear put spreads, 46–47
Bemruda options, 14
bid, 37
binary options, 16
Black-Scholes Model, 23
brokerage accounts, 32–33
brokerage firms, 32–33
bull call spreads, 45–46
butterfly spreads, 48–49
buy to close, 34
buy to open, 34
buy-write, 43–44

C
calendar spreads, 47–48
call options, 6, 11, 12–13
   bull call spreads, 45–46
   buying, 7, 41–42
   covered calls, 43–44
   naked calls, 52–53
   trading, 12–13
   writing (selling), 7
capped-style options, 15–16
cash accounts, 32–33
closing out, 56–57
collars (protective), 53–54
compound options, 16
covered calls, 43–44

Cox-Rubenstein Binomial Option Pricing Model, 22–24

D
day order, 36
delta, 25
discount brokers, 32–33
down-and-in barrier options, 15
down-and-out barrier options, 14

E
European options, 13–14
exercising option, 57
exit strategies, 56–58, 63
exotic options, 14–17
expiration date, 6, 22

F
fill orders, 35
fill or kill order, 36
forward start options, 16

G
gamma, 26
good til cancelled (GTC) order, 36
good til date (GTD) order, 36
Greeks, 25–29

H
hedging, 8–9

I
immediate or cancel order, 36
index options, 17
information sources, 59–61
insurance, 3
in-the-money (ITM), 19–20
intrinsic value, 7, 9–10, 21–22

iron butterfly, 52–53
iron condor, 50–52

L
LEAPS, 16–17
legs, 45
leverage, 3, 8
limit order, 34, 35
Long-term Equity AnticiPation Securities (LEAPS, 16–17
look-back options, 16

M
magazines, 61
making trades, 38
margin accounts, 32–33
margin calls, 33
market conditions, 63
market order, 34, 35
married puts, 44–45
mistakes
    tips for avoiding, 63

N
naked calls, 52–53
newsletters, 60–61
newspapers, 60

O
online resouces, 59
open interest, 37
options
    advantages of, 7–8, 7–9
    American, 13–14
    basics of, 5–10
    buying and selling, 7
    call, 6, 7, 11, 12–13
    defined, 6
    disadvantages of, 9–10
    European, 13–14
    exercising, 57
    exotic, 14–17
    getting started with trading, 31–39
    index, 17
    in-the-money, 19–20
    LEAPS, 16–17
    prices and valuation, 19–24
    put, 6, 11–12
    styles of, 13–17
    types of, 11–13
    vanilla, 13–14
options agreement, 33
options calculator, 39
options chains, 36–37, 39
Options Clearing Corporation (OCC), 31–32
options exchanges, 31
options screener, 39
option symbols, 37
order confirmation, 38
order placement, 34–36
order timing, 35–36
order types, 34–35
out-of-the-money (OTM), 20–21
over-the-counter (OTC) market, 13

P
paper trading, 39
placing trades, 38
premium, 6–7
pricing models, 22–24
protective collars, 53–54
put/call parity, 24
put options, 6, 11–12
    bear put spreads, 46–47
    buying, 7, 42–43
    married puts, 44–45
    trading, 12–13
    writing (selling), 7–9

R
research, 38, 59, 63
rho, 27
risk levels, 9

risk limitation, 8
risk tolerance, 3, 63
rolling out, 57

S

sell to close, 35
sell to open, 35
spreads, 45–49
    bear put, 46–47
    bull call, 45–46
    butterfly, 48–49
    calendar/time, 47–48
    vertical, 45
stocks
    trading, 5
stop-limit order, 35
stop order, 35
straddles (long), 49–50
strangles (long), 54–55
strike price, 6, 11, 14, 37

T

taxes, 10
theta, 28–29
time decay, 6, 10
time spreads, 47–48
time value, 7, 21–22
trade execution, 38
trading accounts, 32–33
trading process, 38
trading strategies, 41–58
    call buying, 41–42
    collars (protective), 53–54
    covered calls, 43–44
    exit strategies, 56–58
    iron butterfly, 51–52
    iron condor, 50–51
    by market outlook, 55–56
    married puts, 44–45
    naked calls, 52–53
    put buying, 42–43
    simple, 41–45
    spreads, 45–49
    straddles (long), 49–50
    strangles (long), 54–55
trading tools, 39

U

up-and-in barrier options, 15
up-and-out barrier options, 15

V

valuation, 19–24
vanilla options, 13–14
vega, 27–28
vertical spreads, 45
volume, 37

W

wasting assets, 10
writing options, 7

Printed in Great Britain
by Amazon